THE HAPPINESS BLUEPRINT

THE HAPPINESS BLUEPRINT

Strategies to Unveil Your True Passion

INNER POWER

Inner Strength Counselling

CONTENTS

CHAPTER 1

Introduction

Lots of folks out there are living their best lives by doing what they truly love. The real winners? They're the ones hustling hard for things they're crazy passionate about. Why? Because when you love what you do, putting in the effort feels more like a joy ride than work.

Ever feel like life's a bit dull or you're not doing what you should be? It might be time to shake things up. Sometimes, there are fears or obstacles blocking the way to your life goals. It's time to tackle those hurdles and turn your dreams into reality.

Many of us aren't exactly sure what gets us fired up. We see successful people going after their dreams, but we're lost about what really lights our fire. Finding that spark is possible, but it means digging deep within yourself. Sometimes, your passion is right in front of you, hidden in plain sight.

Believe it or not, every passion has the potential to pay the bills. It's all about figuring out the right path. Don't let financial worries hold you back from pursuing what you love. You can totally make a living doing what makes your heart sing.

This book is your guide to unlocking your hidden passions. It's loaded with tips to help you explore deep within yourself, pinpoint what drives you, and learn how to turn those passions into reality. With a bit of dedication, your dreams can become more than just dreams – they can become your reality.

By the time you're done with this book, you'll know yourself a whole lot better. You'll pinpoint exactly what lights your fire and have a game plan to make your dreams a reality. All by tapping into your passion and crafting a life that's successful and deeply fulfilling.

CHAPTER 2

Choosing Happiness
Every Day

Feeling unhappy? That's a choice you're making. You hold the reins to your life and the decisions you make. Happiness? It's measured in different ways by different folks. Some link it to money, but truth be told, some wealthy souls are miserably grinding away at something they despise just to make a buck.

Ever gaze at those who seem to have it all? The wealth, the toys, the status? Yet, they're not any happier. Truth is, happiness isn't crafted from external things. It's a choice you make from within.

You'd be surprised—some folks with hefty bank accounts and high positions are downright unhappy. Despite their status, they might be grappling with loneliness, divorce, and more. That happiness you seek? It starts from within. Even those making a fortune might be stuck in jobs they loathe, but they're good at making money nonetheless.

THE SUBJECTIVITY OF HAPPINESS

Happiness—such a subjective concept, isn't it? It's as diverse as each individual's fingerprint.

For some, happiness resides in the heart-pounding excitement of roller coasters or the adrenaline rush of bungee jumping. But for others, these thrilling experiences might resemble pure torment—especially if they grapple with a fear of heights that keeps them far from such daring escapades.

Each person seeks happiness in a unique way. What brings you joy could be your own natural high, something deserving of pursuit. No need to feel wrong about it; your sources of joy are entirely your own. Even if others label it as crazy, remember, it's all due to the subjective nature of happiness.

REDEFINING HAPPINESS

Certainly, some folks seem naturally predisposed to happiness, a trait often rooted in their genetic makeup. Yet, this doesn't condemn those less inclined to eternal joy to a life of perpetual misery. Your happiness, though influenced by genetics, isn't solely bound by this predisposition.

If happiness doesn't come as easily to you, fear not—there's room for change. It's about rewiring the way your mind works and adjusting your daily habits. By consciously adopting behaviors that elevate your happiness quotient, you can learn to brighten your days, welcoming more smiles and embracing a cheerier persona.

POWER OF REST

Undoubtedly, sleep stands as a pivotal component of happiness. It's the body's essential downtime, imperative for optimal functioning. When deprived of adequate rest, moodiness, mental fog, and profound dissatisfaction often loom over our days.

However, getting a full eight hours of sleep doesn't guarantee quality slumber. The issue might lie in oversleeping or sleeping in an uncomfortable manner. Pillow preferences vary greatly among individuals; some may need firmer support while others find comfort in a softer embrace. Even your mattress could significantly impact the quality of your rest.

Sleep deprivation isn't just about feeling groggy—it significantly impacts your overall health. Your journey to holistic well-being demands a consistent, restful night's sleep.

Should sleep issues plague your days and dampen your mood, it's time to address them. Adjusting your daily routine to allow for an earlier bedtime might be necessary. Enlisting support from those around you, especially in a bustling household, could lighten your load and promote better rest.

Difficulty falling asleep could hint at deeper issues like depression. Acknowledging and resolving these sleep challenges are crucial steps towards securing your happiness. Prioritize a good night's rest; it's often the key to brighter, more fulfilling days.

THE JOY OF MOVEMENT

Physical exercise is a powerful ally for your body and mind, as it triggers the release of endorphins, the happiness-inducing chemicals in your brain. Its significance goes beyond physical health; it contributes to holistic well-being.

Adopting an exercise routine need not be a daunting task requiring heavy workouts every day. The goal is to aim for some form of daily physical activity that induces perspiration. Surprisingly, everyday activities like cleaning the house or engaging in household chores can serve as excellent workouts. It's not just about shedding pounds; it's about cultivating joy and contentment.

INNER PEACE

Engaging in meditation doesn't imply being part of a cult or going against any religious beliefs. Some associate meditation solely with Buddhism, often considering it incorrect. However, they overlook a valuable practice that could significantly bring balance to their lives.

Meditation stands as one of the most impactful methods to enhance your personal well-being. Medical experts have confirmed its ability to stimulate brain activity on the left side, triggering positive emotions within the body.

CHAPTER 3

Self-Discovery

When seeking happiness or attempting to bridge the gap in your life, the quest for your true passion becomes imperative. Numerous probing questions hold the key to unraveling this journey and understanding yourself better. These questions can potentially illuminate the barriers hindering your happiness and pursuit of your passions. Below are several queries worth pondering. Grab a notepad or mentally note down your responses—jotting them down tends to yield better insights.

EXPLORING PERSONAL SPARKS

Discovering what genuinely inspires and captivates you might be a challenging question to address. Often, the answer may unfold after pondering the subsequent questions. Nevertheless, it's crucial to be precise about the sources of your inspiration. What specific elements or experiences ignite your enthusiasm? Identify the aspects or activities that truly engage and exhilarate you.

Pursue Fearlessly

Imagine a scenario where failure is not an option. What would you pursue if you were guaranteed success? Fear of failure often prevents people from engaging in certain activities. However, if the possibility of failure was completely eliminated, what endeavor would you wholeheartedly embrace without hesitation?

Reimagining Your Path

If given the chance to start anew, would you tread the same path or venture into uncharted territories? Many individuals find themselves trapped in routines that provide little joy or fulfillment. If presented with a clean slate, would you seize the opportunity to forge a new direction, or would you revisit your current trajectory?

Financial Limits

If financial constraints were no longer a concern, what aspirations would you chase? Countless individuals harbor dreams they yearn to pursue but find themselves held back by monetary limitations. Imagine a world where money is no barrier—what endeavors would you embark upon, unrestricted by financial constraints?

Ultimate Dream

What's the grand vision that fuels your aspirations? Amidst life's chaos, there's often one profound dream that beckons us. Focus on that singular aspiration that sets your heart ablaze.

Break Down Barriers

Understanding and articulating the barriers hindering your dreams is a crucial process in breaking their hold over you. Recognizing the elements that prevent you from pursuing your aspirations allows you to confront and eventually dismantle them.

These barriers could manifest in various forms - from external factors like lack of financial support, unsupportive relationships, or a fear of failure to internal struggles such as self-doubt, lack of skill or confidence, or a reluctance to leave the comfort zone.

By acknowledging these barriers, you open the door to finding solutions. It's about addressing each obstacle methodically, seeking solutions, and gaining confidence in your ability to overcome them. Identifying these roadblocks is the first step toward crafting strategies to surmount them and propel yourself toward your dreams.

Unveiling Hidden Passions

Lots of folks harbor aspirations and interests they're hesitant to disclose, fearing ridicule from others. There might be a passion you hold back because you worry it might seem trivial or ridiculous to others. What is this passion you hesitate to reveal?

Childhood Dreams

Recall your childhood aspirations. Were there dreams you held onto as a child that haven't yet come to fruition? Do you contemplate what it might have been like if you pursued those childhood dreams? If given the chance, would you embark on that path now?

Reflections on Life's Regrets and Aspirations

Consider what you'd regret not doing if faced with a limited time left. Many individuals harbor regrets as life nears its end, wishing they'd pursued certain dreams. If given only a few weeks to live, what would your regrets be? What aspirations would you long to fulfill?

These reflections provide insights into your sources of happiness and dreams. Imagine winning the lottery—what would you do? Understanding these aspirations is crucial for shaping your path forward.

CHAPTER 4

Unveiling Hidden
Talents and Past Joys

Discovering and capitalizing on your existing talents and peak experiences are instrumental in steering your dreams toward reality. These moments can boost your confidence and serve as a foundation for success.

Reflect on your peak experiences—the moments in life where you shone brightly or felt most fulfilled. They needn't be award-winning events but rather instances of pure enjoyment and accomplishment. Consider past achievements or times when you felt elated. Perhaps you enjoyed building or creating things when you were younger.

Your current talents are assets to achieve your goals. These skills might include organization, marketing, or hidden abilities waiting to be uncovered. Even simple tasks like event announcements, making calls, gardening, or baking can be valuable skills.

You don't necessarily need expert-level talents. Your knowledge and interests can be your forte. Maybe you possess extensive knowledge on a subject purely out of personal interest, not professional necessity.

Consider resurrecting past passions that once filled your life with joy. Perhaps you were a runner with aspirations to conquer the New York City Marathon but later abandoned the dream due to lifestyle changes. Don't let past hindrances block the pursuit of your dreams—rediscover your aspirations and strive for them again.

Everyone has a skill or something they excel at, even if it's not a traditional hobby. If you haven't identified your skill yet, explore what interests you the most. Often, people excel when they truly enjoy what they do.

CHAPTER 5

Unleashing Passion through Curiosity

Curiosity acts as the catalyst for passion, serving as a gateway to understanding what truly drives you. Sometimes, misconceptions or barriers hinder the realization of our genuine passions. Here are various ways to harness curiosity in uncovering your true passion, propelling you toward success.

AGILE MIND THROUGH CURIOSITY

Embracing curiosity nurtures mental agility. It inspires continuous questioning and pursuit of answers, fostering an active and resilient mind. Just as exercise strengthens muscles, engaging curiosity fortifies the brain, enhancing its strength and adaptability.

Embracing Novel Perspectives

Curiosity is the gateway to diverse viewpoints. When you're confined to one perspective, your options become limited. Similarly, if you perceive your life as unchangeable, it may hinder your success. Opening yourself to new ideas broadens your possibilities.

Curiosity not only generates ideas but also enables you to acknowledge and consider them. Without curiosity, crucial ideas might slip away unnoticed. It's crucial to remain receptive to suggestions, even those you might initially resist. Being open to suggestions involves asking questions and exploring varied answers.

Unveiling Hidden Opportunities

An open mind reveals a broader spectrum of possibilities in every circumstance. Embracing curiosity allows you to perceive the world in a way that transcends the ordinary. You'll uncover realms and opportunities beyond the surface, enabling you to wield your curious mind to manifest these hidden prospects.

Infusing Life with Excitement

Curiosity breathes life into the mundane, igniting excitement within your daily experiences. Embracing curiosity unveils a world teeming with novelties and fascinations, from gadgets to hidden wonders waiting to be discovered. By nurturing a curious spirit, life transforms into an adventure, allowing you to break free from routine and explore the extraordinary in the ordinary.

Embracing Curiosity

Nurturing curiosity breathes life into every moment, transforming the mundane into an exciting journey. Developing curiosity is key to revamping life's routine and uncovering the hidden treasures within it. Here's how to cultivate a more inquisitive spirit:

1. **Keep an Open Mind**: Embrace different viewpoints and challenge your usual way of thinking. Exploring various perspectives can unleash new possibilities and broaden your horizons.
2. **Avoid Taking Things for Granted**: Dive deeper into life's seemingly simple aspects. Cherish moments, avoid wasting time, and relish the significance of seemingly trivial experiences.
3. **Ask Questions**: Never hesitate to inquire. Questions unveil hidden depths and open doors to understanding people, situations, and the world around you.
4. **Learn Continuously**: Explore new areas of knowledge, encouraging a lifelong learning mentality. Confront learning as an exciting endeavor that enriches your pursuit of passions.

5. **Find Joy in Learning**: Approach learning as an enjoyable journey toward your goals. Regardless of age, treat every opportunity to learn as an adventure.

6. **Make the Mundane Fun**: Reframe tasks or activities that seem mundane into exciting challenges. Infuse excitement into the routine by looking at things differently.

7. **Expand Reading Horizons**: Explore various topics through reading to fuel your curiosity. Even if you have a primary interest, branching out can broaden your perspective.

By embracing curiosity, you embark on a journey of continuous learning and discovery, enriching your life and uncovering passions you might not have realized existed.

CULTIVATING CREATIVITY

Feeling Non-Creative?

Ever felt you lacked creativity, even though you thought you had it? To turn your passions into reality, nurturing creativity is vital. You'll need to creatively overcome barriers and transform ideas into action. The more creative you get, the more successful your journey will be. Here are strategies to enhance your creativity.

Game of Creativity

Transform every situation into a game. Set rules, and objectives, and identify obstacles. The more creatively you solve these challenges, the more successful you become.

Goal-Driven Creativity

Set goals with deadlines. Attach deadlines to tasks to infuse excitement and reduce procrastination. Deadlines make tasks more engaging and focused.

Self-Expression and Creativity

Embrace opportunities for self-expression creatively. Be it your dinner presentation or a workplace presentation, seek every chance to express yourself uniquely.

Focus and Creativity

Minimize distractions and noise to enhance focus. Immersed focus reveals hidden opportunities and qualities in tasks. If something seems boring, find ways to make it engaging.

Big Picture Vision

View dull activities as smaller parts of a larger picture. Understanding the broader context of tasks enhances creativity and fuels enthusiasm for every aspect.

TAKE A HOME TOUR

Your home holds clues to your true passions. Often, the items we collect or surround ourselves with mirror our interests. Take a stroll through your abode and observe your decorations, collections, or hobbies. These items might reveal your hidden passions.

Exploring your living space might unravel hidden clues about your true passions. Your possessions, be they collectibles, artwork, or books, often reflect your interests, serving as a roadmap to your true calling.

Surprisingly, the items adorning your home may subtly echo your genuine passions. These could range from collectibles adorning shelves to the hobbies you indulge in during leisure moments. Your home might hold the key to discovering your overlooked interests.

CHAPTER 6

Obstacles

Often, individuals know their true passions but face external obstacles hindering their pursuit. If external barriers block your path to realizing your dreams, it's crucial to navigate beyond them. You wield the power to overcome these impediments and take charge of your journey towards your aspirations.

SUPPORTIVE CIRCLES

External opinions, particularly negative ones, often serve as the biggest blockade preventing individuals from pursuing their passions. When met with ridicule or discouragement from others, it can be challenging to stay motivated.

Surrounding yourself with supportive individuals is vital. Those who diminish your aspirations or belittle your dreams shouldn't have a place in your support network. If a spouse or family member doesn't back your passion, it's essential to communicate the importance of their support. However, prioritizing your dreams over unsupportive opinions is crucial for your fulfillment.

Having a supportive circle empowers you to achieve anything. In cases where loved ones lack emotional support, asserting your commitment to your dreams becomes pivotal. While temporarily distancing yourself might be necessary, making it clear that your dreams bring happiness can help them understand and eventually support your journey.

OVERCOMING FINANCIAL HURDLES

Money often stands as a significant barrier that deters individuals from pursuing their passions, especially when it comes to funding dreams. Whether it's starting a business or pursuing a costly endeavor, financial constraints can indeed be conquered with strategic planning.

Initiating cost-cutting measures in your daily life is an effective way to save money for your passion. Simple changes, like packing lunch instead of eating out or finding alternative commuting options, can accumulate savings over time. Every penny saved counts towards funding your dream.

Furthermore, getting creative in your approach might reveal various avenues to generate additional income or even kickstart your dream without hefty initial costs. Starting a home-based business or an online venture could be a viable option.

Sometimes, an online business can surpass the success of a physical store.

Although money can seem like a daunting obstacle, it shouldn't be the reason to abandon your dreams. Consider seeking support from a supportive spouse or exploring alternate means of funding your passion. Often, the payoff and fulfillment derived from living out your dreams outweigh the initial financial challenges.

MANAGING TIME EFFECTIVELY

Lack of time is a common refrain for those unable to pursue their passions. While commitments like work and family can be demanding, finding time for your dreams is crucial for personal fulfillment.

To overcome time constraints, consider making small adjustments to your daily routine. Waking up slightly earlier or utilizing your lunch hour to engage in your passion can make a significant difference. However, it's essential not to compromise your sleep, as rest is crucial for overall well-being.

Often, time gets frittered away on non-essential activities like excessive TV watching or aimless socializing. Identifying and cutting down on these time drains can free up hours that could be dedicated to your passion. Manage your leisure time more efficiently to create space for your interests without sacrificing relaxation entirely.

When it comes to pursuing your passion, remember that progress doesn't have to happen all at once. Even dedicating a small amount of time daily can accumulate and move your project forward. Breaking down tasks into manageable chunks ensures consistent progress while keeping you motivated.

Ultimately, it's about recognizing that time can be found if you're willing to reprioritize and manage it effectively. By making deliberate choices and eliminating time-wasting activities, you can carve out precious moments to dedicate to your passion.

ALIGNING PASSION WITH WORK

If your current job stifles your ability to pursue your passions, it might be time for a change. It's essential to work towards finding a role that aligns with your passions and brings you fulfillment. However, simply switching employers might not address the root cause if the new role doesn't resonate with your interests.

The key is to seek a career that genuinely inspires you. When you're passionate about your work, success naturally follows. Happiness at work significantly impacts productivity and job satisfaction. If your current role doesn't evoke enthusiasm, it's challenging to excel or progress.

Reflect on what truly motivates and excites you professionally. What skills or activities bring you joy? Identifying these elements can guide you toward a career path that aligns with your passions.

Transitioning to a job that resonates with your interests might not be an overnight process. It often involves planning, upskilling, networking, and perhaps even taking small steps toward your dream while still employed.

Ultimately, your job shouldn't be a hindrance to your happiness. Striving for a role that fuels your passion will not only make waking up each morning more enjoyable but will also contribute significantly to your overall contentment and success.

OVERCOMING FEAR OF FAILURE

Fear often stands as a significant obstacle on the path toward pursuing passions and achieving dreams. However, it's crucial to understand that fear can be overcome. Curiosity and openness to new ideas can help challenge the limitations imposed by fear and allow for the possibility of better outcomes.

The fear of failure is a common barrier that prevents many from taking steps toward their passions. It's natural to fear failure, much like learning something new or riding a bicycle for the first time. Progress in any pursuit usually involves encountering failures along the way. Embracing these setbacks as learning experiences rather than insurmountable roadblocks is key. Each failure offers a chance for growth and learning, helping to build resilience and determination.

It's important not to let the fear of failure hinder progress. Instead, view failures as stepping stones towards eventual success. Transforming failure into a positive learning experience enables personal growth and development.

Surprisingly, some individuals fear success as much as they fear failure. This fear might manifest in self-sabotaging behaviors, like spending savings set aside for dreams on unnecessary things. Often, these actions stem from low self-esteem and a belief that success is beyond one's capabilities.

It's crucial to acknowledge that being successful is attainable if you believe in yourself. Don't let the fear of success limit your potential. You have the ability to be as successful as you believe you can be. Overcoming this fear involves nurturing self-confidence and realizing that success is within reach with determination and effort. Don't allow fear to hold you back from reaching your fullest potential.

PERPETUAL LEARNING

The misconception that learning ends after completing formal education often holds people back from pursuing their passions. Regardless of age or stage in life, the capacity to learn remains constant. Even at an elderly age, one can continue learning and growing. It's essential to embrace the idea that learning is an ongoing, exciting process.

Embrace Learning for Passion Pursuits

When pursuing your passions, sometimes acquiring new knowledge or certifications might be necessary. Rather than seeing these requirements as obstacles, view them as stepping stones toward achieving your dreams. Each new learning experience becomes a valuable tool on your journey to realizing your aspirations.

Overcoming Perceived Barriers

Barriers are often perceived as insurmountable obstacles, deterring individuals from pursuing their passions. However, these barriers, whether financial, educational, or circumstantial, are temporary challenges. Recognizing that you have control over these barriers and the power to overcome them creatively is crucial. Whether it's finding alternative funding sources or leveraging existing skills, barriers can be navigated with creativity and determination.

Taking Charge of Your Dreams

It's important to assert control over the barriers that stand in the way of your passions. By taking charge of your life and rejecting these barriers as excuses, you pave the way for living out your dreams. Stand firm and determined in your pursuit, refusing to let temporary hindrances hold you back from what you truly desire.

CHAPTER 7

Set a Goal

Importance of Setting Goals

Setting goals is crucial for several reasons. It not only allows you to track progress but also provides a sense of anticipation and cultivates ambition. Without setting clear objectives, achieving your dreams becomes significantly more challenging.

Attaching Deadlines and Milestones

Assigning specific completion dates to your goals is key. Break down your overarching goal into smaller milestones, each with its own estimated deadline. This step-by-step approach enables you to track your progress and maintain focus. While these dates may not always align perfectly, they offer guidance and a structured path toward your ultimate goal.

Creating Anticipation and Progress

Setting goals gives you something to look forward to. Establishing deadlines and milestones keeps you motivated and ensures that your aspirations feel more tangible. Tracking your progress visually, such as with charts outlining each step, allows you to see how far you've come and how much closer you are to realizing your dream.

Fueling Ambition

As you approach your ultimate passion, your ambition naturally intensifies. If achieving your goal requires refining your skills, don't hesitate to take relevant classes or workshops. Viewing these learning experiences as vital steps in your journey helps mark progress and brings you nearer to your aspiration.

Rewarding Progress and Hard Work

When you reach significant milestones or complete challenging steps, it's important to reward yourself. Recognize your hard work and dedication by celebrating these achievements. Whether it's taking a night off or indulging in a treat, acknowledging your progress encourages continued effort.

Measuring Success and Progress

Approaching each project or dream as a series of goals with clear steps make the path seem more manageable. This structured approach not only motivates you to work harder but also allows you to gauge how close you are to fulfilling your long-held dreams. Tracking progress empowers you to see the concrete steps you've taken toward your goal.

By setting attainable goals, breaking them down into manageable steps, and rewarding yourself along the way, you create a roadmap to success and pave the way for making your dreams a reality.

CHAPTER 8

Success Beyond Wealth

Success isn't solely defined by money; it's measured by personal fulfillment. Pursuing your passions leads to success in different ways. While monetary gains might follow, the key lies in engaging with what truly drives you. When you work on something you're deeply passionate about, financial success often accompanies it. However, the true essence of success is reflected in the satisfaction of looking back on life, knowing you've pursued your dreams without regrets.

EMBRACE EVERY PART

Your passion should be fulfilling and all-encompassing. It's crucial to embrace every facet of it, not just the obvious parts. Find joy in the complete experience, even the less ideal moments, like delays when ordering parts. Rather than seeing setbacks as signs to abandon your passion, view them as opportunities; for instance, use a delay to enjoy a mini-vacation. Don't let negative incidents discourage you. Stay authentic and true to yourself in every aspect of pursuing your passion.

AUTHENTIC PASSION

Genuine passion doesn't require a show for others; it stems from within. When you deeply love what you do, passion flows naturally. It's reflected in your work; for instance, if you craft clay pots, you'll ensure each pot is flawless before sending it out. This dedication arises from pride and ownership—your name is on every creation, making you proud of every detail.

LEADERSHIP

To live your dream, embracing leadership is crucial. It's about showcasing how to transform your life, not simply following others' paths. Be passionate about driving change in your life. Forge your vision and pave the path by achieving the goals you've set for yourself.

STRIVING FOR PROGRESS

While pursuing your passion, perfection won't happen instantly. Embrace continuous improvement by refining methods that slow you down or yield unsatisfactory results. Over time, this commitment will lead to noticeable enhancements in your work.

Initially, expect chaos and disorder in your pursuit. Trial and error will be your companions; you might repeat attempts numerous times before crafting the most efficient and high-quality approach. Yet, persisting through these challenges will ultimately refine your process.

EMBRACING ACTION

In the realm of pursuing your passion, action is key. Combatting procrastination requires constant action—setting reminders, seeking support from action-oriented individuals, and acknowledging progress.

To sidestep procrastination, maintain focus on your dream by consistently taking action. Keep visual reminders, like signs, to reinforce your commitment to working towards your passion.

It's crucial to assemble a team that shares your action-oriented mindset. While a supportive aunt may not contribute to task-oriented work, she might excel in generating enthusiasm or support. Recognize and appreciate the efforts of those aiding your journey, even if it's through verbal appreciation rather than monetary rewards.

CHAPTER 9

Transforming Passion into Reality

Bringing your passions to life involves several crucial steps. Once you've identified and embraced your passion, the next phase is to turn it into a tangible reality. Here are actionable steps you can take to make your dreams a reality.

THE POWER OF BELIEF

Belief is the cornerstone of success. Your confidence in your abilities shapes your journey toward success. Without belief, your endeavors may falter. It's not about proving yourself to others; it's about believing in yourself. Embrace the belief in your success silently but fervently. Envision yourself achieving your goals and sharing your story on platforms like the Oprah Winfrey Show. Let belief empower your thoughts and actions towards making your passion a reality.

POSITIVITY

Your attitude holds the key to your success. Maintaining a positive outlook is crucial when pursuing your passion. Embrace positivity in every aspect of your journey. Let setbacks be stepping stones for learning and growth. Your positive mindset will fuel your success in both your business and your passion.

A positive attitude is a catalyst for success. It influences your belief in yourself and your endeavors. When you radiate positivity, the universe often aligns in your favor. Remember, it's not about how dire a situation seems but how your attitude shapes it. Your positivity will transform challenges into opportunities for growth.

REFINING YOUR VISION

When your passion seems out of reach, refine your idea instead of abandoning it. Use this time to perfect your plan. Dive into the details of your project or business endeavor. Every moment, even the waiting periods, offers an opportunity to enhance your vision. Don't let delays deter you; view them as chances to fortify your intentions and refine your strategy.

IGNITE ACTION

Initiating action swiftly is pivotal in propelling your passion forward. Act promptly on your ideas without waiting for opportunities to come to you. Similarly, tackle problems promptly. This proactive approach fosters an unbreakable momentum, eradicating any tendencies of procrastination and fostering heightened productivity.

RESOURCES

Utilize all available resources to ensure progress toward your goals. If funds are limited, seek assistance from friends or supportive individuals for services like daycare or essential errands. Engage your creativity to tackle resource shortages effectively. For instance, if you lack the necessary tools or equipment, explore alternative sources or communal spaces such as public libraries for access. Stay resourceful to advance your passion towards success.

EMBRACING SACRIFICE AND HARD WORK

Working towards your passion often demands immense sacrifice and unwavering dedication.

Initially, when embarking on your journey, financial struggles might be prevalent. Overnight success is unrealistic, but the key is doing what you love. To achieve your dreams, long hours and sacrificing family time become inevitable. Sacrifice is a pivotal aspect of the road to success.

There's no substitute for hard work when striving for your goals. Your success lies in your hands, requiring persistent and strenuous efforts. Embrace the toil, late hours, and challenges, for they pave the way to a fulfilling reward in the end.

STRUCTURING YOUR LIFE

To ensure success in your newfound endeavor, align your life around your passion. Crafting a fulfilling routine sets the tone for a triumphant day. Start your mornings early, savor a cup of coffee, peruse the news, engage with your blog, and more. Construct a day that nurtures your well-being and amplifies productivity.

Design your schedule to incorporate ample exercise and wholesome choices. Adequate sleep is paramount; while hard work is necessary, neglecting sleep jeopardizes your ability to relish your passion. Striking a balance is essential—working towards your passion involves getting proper rest. Effective organization paves the way for success and heightened productivity.

VISUALIZATION AND MEDITATION

Visualization and meditation serve as crucial tools in your pursuit of your passion. These practices aid in envisioning the path toward your aspirations. By visualizing your goals and meditating on them, you allow your ideas to take shape within you, solidifying your commitment to realizing them. Manifest your desires through these practices and pave the way to making them a tangible reality.

CHAPTER 10

The Essence of Living Your Passion

Living your true passion involves embracing a few crucial elements: wholehearted dedication, freedom from focusing on outcomes, and transcending survival concerns.

Dedication to Your Passion: Dedicate your time and energy to your passion. Being wholly committed and invested in your pursuit sets the foundation for success.

Pain and Pleasure: Recognize that while your passion may bring joy, achieving your goals may involve pain and frustration. Embrace the challenges as part of the journey, understanding that they contribute to soul satisfaction in the long run.

Detachment from Results: Focus on the journey rather than fixating solely on the outcome. Trust in the process, allowing the universe to unfold as it should.

Release Survival Worries: Let go of fears and worries about survival. Cultivate courage and positivity, knowing that you possess the power to navigate challenges and thrive in pursuit of your passion.

CHAPTER 11

A Path to Fulfilment

Discovering and pursuing your passion is a gateway to a fulfilling life, and success is not merely measured by financial wealth but by the pursuit of what truly ignites your soul.

To find your passion, self-reflection is key. Ask yourself probing questions and observe the clues scattered around you. Often, your genuine passion may be subtly evident in your surroundings.

Obstacles may hinder your path, but remember, you can overcome them. With determination, anyone can turn their passion into a thriving personal enterprise.

The core principles of making your passion a reality involve unwavering belief in your ability to succeed and dedicated hard work. Effort breeds success, and even during waiting periods, meticulous planning can lay the groundwork for your future endeavors.

Setting goals with achievable milestones is pivotal. Monitoring progress and rewarding achievements along the way not only fuels motivation but also provides a tangible roadmap toward your aspirations.

Ultimately, your worthiness to live your passion is undeniable. You possess the same potential as anyone else, deserving of happiness and the fulfillment of your deepest passions.